ROBOT WORLD

Contents

Badger

Vocabulary

astronauts	International Space Station
communicate	robotic
digital	sensor
equipment	trophy

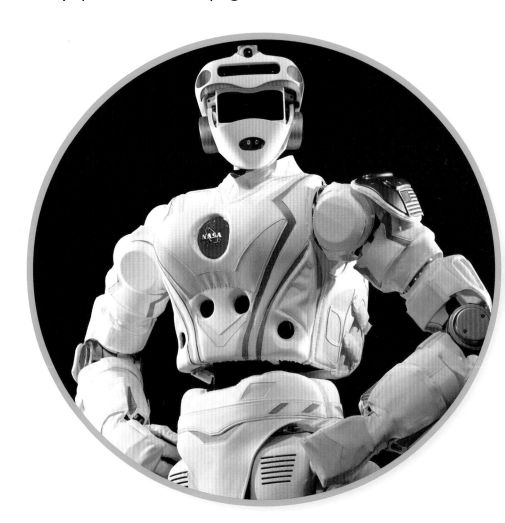

1. Meet the robots

If you think robots are only found in science fiction books and films, then you are wrong.

All around the world, robots are becoming a part of daily life.

Robots can do everything, from cleaning up your mess to looking after you when you are ill.

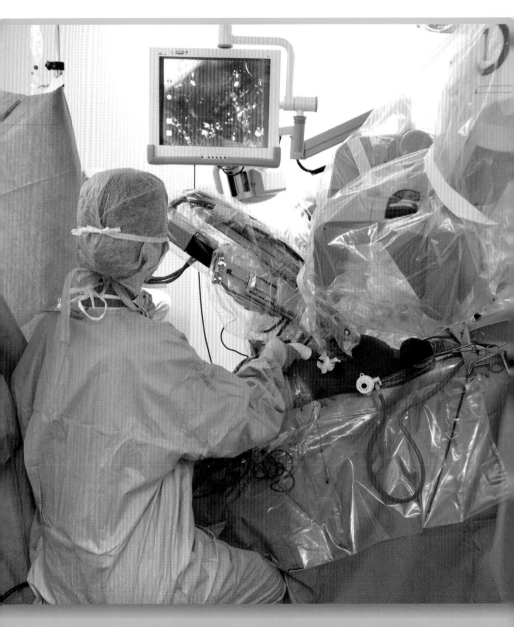

Some people even have robotic hands or legs!

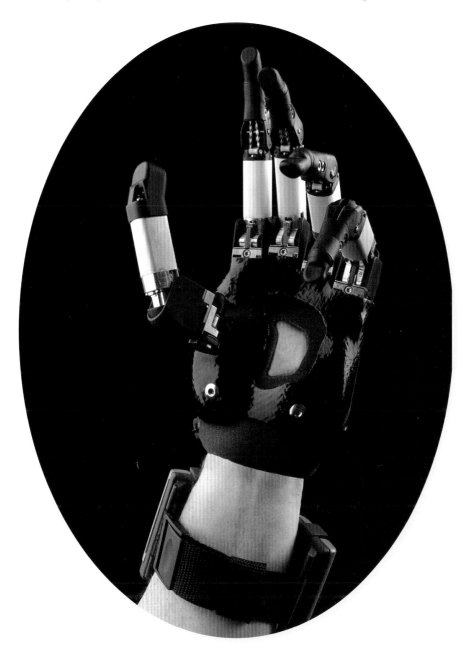

2. Home robots

Did you know you can already buy robots to help with housework?

Robot vacuum cleaners glide across the floor, sucking up dirt.

These robots use digital cameras to stop them bumping into furniture or falling down stairs.

This clever robot can stick to glass so it can clean the windows. How does it not fall off?

Some robots can help you
with your shopping.

Budgee is a three-wheeled robot
that follows you around.

How does it do that?

You carry a sensor in your pocket.

Budgee can carry your shopping in its basket.

If you leave Budgee behind by mistake, it sends a message to your mobile phone!

3. Medical robots

Some robots can even look after ill people.

Doctors and nurses sometimes hurt their backs lifting people out of bed in hospitals.

RoNA has been designed to help. Its name stands for Robotic Nursing Assistant.
It can carry patients using its strong mechanical arms.

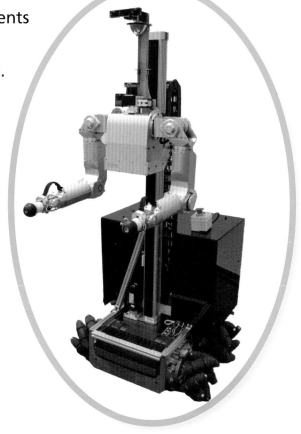

Serbot is a smaller version of RoNA that can be used at home. This robot can help disabled people to stand up.

It can also check the health of the person it is looking after.

WOW! facts

Patients can even talk to a doctor using the screen in Serbot's chest.

4 Traffic robots

We are used to seeing traffic lights on the road but have you ever seen a traffic robot?

These giant robots control the traffic in a country in Africa.

Drivers watch for the coloured lights on the robot's arms and body.

Red means stop and green means go.

The robots watch the drivers too!

Each robot has four cameras ready to spot anyone driving too fast!

5. Space robots

In 2013, Kirobo became the first robot to talk in space.

It was sent to the International Space Station to see how robots can communicate with humans.

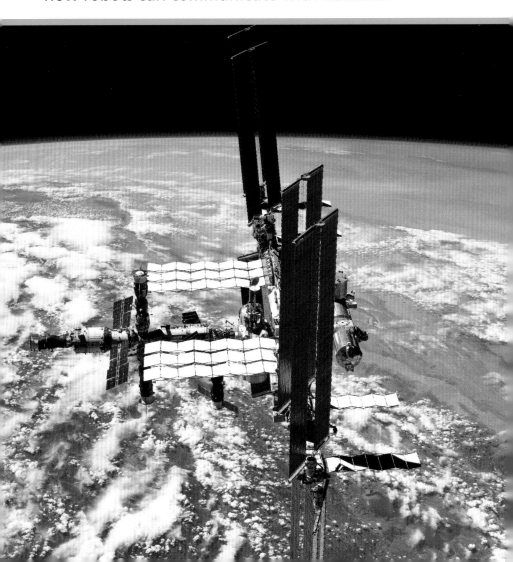

Kirobo understands questions and can choose the right words for its answers.

It even recognises people's faces so it knows who it is talking to.

Kirobo's first words in space were:"Good morning to everyone on Earth. This is Kirobo. I am the world's first talking robot astronaut. Nice to meet you."

In future, larger robots may be sent into space. Walking robots are already being built for missions to the planet Mars.

The robots will arrive long before human astronauts so they can start building landing sites and places for the astronauts to live.

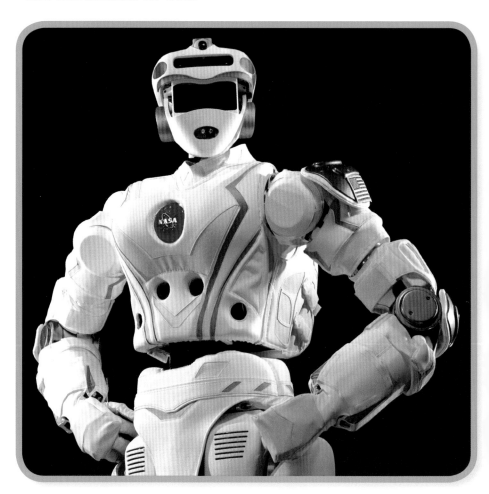

6. Animal robots

Not all robots are based on humans.

Swarm robots are tiny machines that work together in a group, like ants.

If one swarm robot goes wrong, another robot just takes its place.

Swarms of robots could be used in places that are too dangerous for humans.

Robots based on snakes or worms are already used at disaster sites.

The Active Scope Camera is a robot that looks like a worm. It can crawl into buildings that have fallen down.

The camera on this robot is used to find people trapped in the rubble.

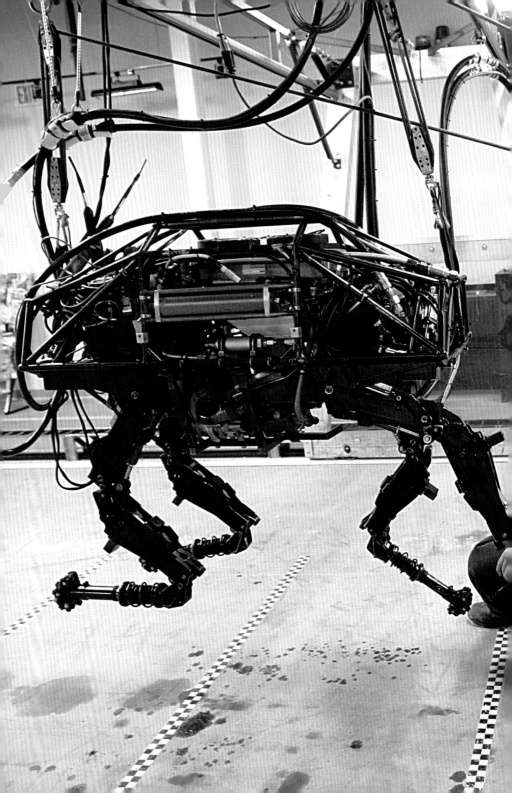

Most robots can't walk on rough or muddy ground.

But BigDog can!

This robot walks on four legs like a dog and can carry heavy equipment on its back.

BigDog can even run, but only at two miles per hour.

WildCat is much faster. It runs like a cheetah and can reach speeds of 16 miles per hour.

That's twice as fast as a human!

You've heard of the football World Cup, but what about the Robocup?

Every year, teams of football-playing robots from around the world compete to win the Robocup trophy.

Some of the robot teams roll around on wheels, while others move like humans. These small robot players can kick, jump and throw balls.

The organisers of Robocup dream of a time when a team of robot footballers beats a team of humans.

They think that this could happen by 2050.

7. Human robots

In 2006, Nigel Ackland lost his hand in an accident at work.

Six years later, it was replaced by an amazing robotic hand.

Nigel's robotic hand is controlled using the muscles in his upper arm and moves just like a real hand.

It works so well that Nigel can peel vegetables, type on a computer and even tie his own shoelaces again.

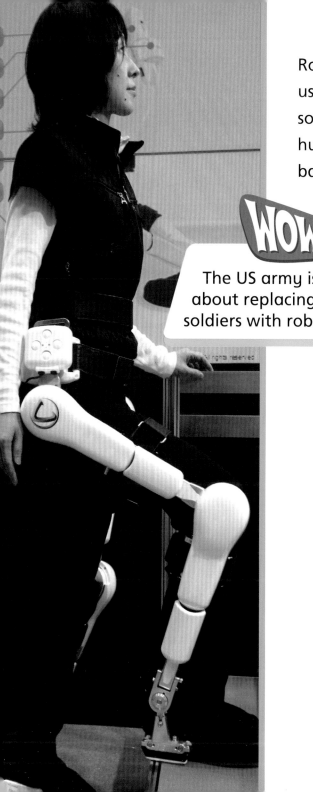

Robotic legs are used to help soldiers who have hurt their legs in battle.

WOW! facts

The US army is thinking about replacing 25% of its soldiers with robots by 2040.

Robots are improving all the time.

Who knows what they will do next?

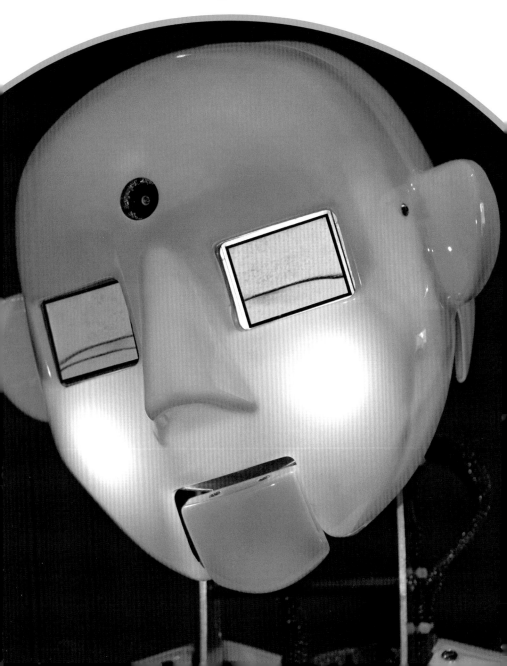

Questions

What is the name of the robot that can help with your shopping? *(pages 10 and 11)*

Where in the world can you find a traffic robot? *(page 14)*

What is the name of the robot that went to the International Space Station? *(pages 16 and 17)*

How fast can the BigDog robot run? *(page 23)*

What is the name of the robot World Cup? *(pages 25 and 26)*

If you could build a robot, what would you make it do?

Index